A CHRISTIAN'S GUIDE
TO THE
NEW TESTAMENT

A CHRISTIAN'S GUIDE
TO THE
NEW TESTAMENT

By

ALAN COLE

MOODY PRESS • CHICAGO

Contents

1 WHAT IS THE GOSPEL?

This question is far more basic than the secondary question "What are the Gospels?", although we shall ask that later. What we want to find out now is: What was the gospel preached, before the Gospel books were written? Our reasons are twofold: first, all the books of the New Testament clearly contain this same gospel. Indeed, it is only because they contain it that we have a 'New Testament' which is a unity, instead of a mere collection of books about God. Secondly, this 'gospel', first as taught by Christ during His earthly ministry, and then as taught by His followers, in the days of the Acts of the Apostles, clearly came before the writing of Matthew, Mark, Luke and John. Of course, we do not mean that it will be different from the gospel message in these Gospel books; but it will be a sort of 'iron rations', or 'basic gospel', teaching us what things are central. Is there any way in which we can discover it?

□ Gospel Talks

One of the easiest ways to see what it was (and thus, incidentally, to see whether we preach it today or not) is to look at some of the earliest recorded 'Gospel Talks' or 'Evangelistic Meetings' in the New Testament. You will find them in the opening chapters of the Acts of the Apostles, beginning immediately after the coming of the Holy Spirit at Pentecost (Acts 2). Before that time, you could scarcely expect to find full 'Christian' preaching by the apostles, although they had long been 'disciples' and 'followers' of Jesus. But it was only as God's Holy Spirit, the Spirit promised by the Lord Jesus to His disciples (John 14: 16), brought all past acts and words of Jesus to their remembrance (John 14: 26) and taught them the true meaning, that they could even see the gospel for themselves—let alone preach it to others.

□ Church Campaigns

We should however remember that these early 'Gospel Talks' were preached to Jews, not Gentiles. That is almost the same as saying, in modern terms, that Peter was conducting an 'Evangelistic Campaign' directed at 'church members', not 'outsiders'. We all know that it is just as essential to preach conversion inside the church as it is outside; but we also know that we use very different language and illustrations. With churchgoers, we can assume

8

that they know much more about God with their heads at least, if not in their hearts. What we want is response to truth already known, and that is exactly the response which Peter wants to obtain from his hearers.

□ They Were There

We should also remember that these 'sermons' were really heart-to-heart talks addressed directly to men who had seen Jesus, heard His teaching, seen some at least of His miracles—and shouted for His death in front of Pilate. They were the very men who had rejected and killed the Prince of Life; and therefore the sermons have a personal thrust and force like that of Nathan the prophet before King David (2 Samuel 12). This means that Peter will appeal directly to their knowledge of Christ and His words and deeds—and also appeal directly to their consciences. But there is really no difference here from our position: we know of the words and deeds of Christ, just as they did—though our knowledge is from the pages of the New Testament, which the men of that generation wrote, under the guidance and inspiration of the Holy Spirit. Further, each one of us (unless we believe in Jesus) is just as guilty of crucifying Christ as any of the Jews who surged around the Cross. The Negro spiritual that says, 'Were you there, when they crucified my Lord?' contains a great deal of truth; and the answer is, 'Yes—I was'.

□ Peter's Sermon

Let us now look at one of the passages. You will find it in Peter's sermon on the Day of Pentecost (Acts 2: 22 ff.). Peter has already explained that what the Jews have seen and heard is God's fulfilment of the promises of the Old Testament; and now he seizes the opportunity to preach the gospel. He begins by telling them of Jesus of Nazareth; they must be familiar with His name at least. More, they must recognise that He was no ordinary Person—He was someone specially singled out by God. Why, they all know the stories of His miracles and signs; and these could only be God working through Him. But He had been 'given up' to the Jews by one of His own followers; the Jews, in their turn, had deliberately used heathen Gentiles to kill Him upon a cross. Peter explains that, while in one sense this was the sin of Jews and Gentiles alike, in another sense, this did not take God by surprise: indeed, it was His deliberate will and plan. Further, the Cross was not the end: God raised Jesus to life again, for Jesus, by His very Nature, was not the sort of person Whom death could hold. To prove this, Peter appeals confidently to God's Word, as contained in the Psalms: this passage shows clearly that Jesus is the Messiah Whom the Jews should have been awaiting—the 'Christ', God's 'anointed' Son and Servant. If some puzzled Jews should question the fact that He rose again from the dead, Peter can point to all the apostles as men that met the risen Christ, and can thus bear witness to the truth of the resurrection. More, He not only rose from the dead: He went up in triumph to the very presence of God. God, in fact, gave Him peculiar honour, because of what He had done. God gave Him the gift of the Holy Spirit for men; and that very day, He had given mankind that gift. More, His final triumph, though delayed, is now sure: He has only to wait until God finally subdues His foes, and He reigns without a rival. Finally, Peter brings home the personal guilt of his Jewish listeners by reminding them that it is they who have crucified the One Whom God has shown to be both Christ and God (or 'Lord').

□ Peter's Sermon-Headings

Now, this seems to us a very simple outline of the gospel: it tells of the life, death, resurrection, and ultimate triumph of the Lord Jesus. It tells both of the guilt of man, and of God's wonderful gift of the Spirit; and, best of all, it tells of a risen Jesus Whom men may meet and know for themselves, as the apostles did. It is true that this is not complete; but it is the core of the gospel, and we shall recognise it everywhere in the New Testament.

□ The Hearers' Response

Let us now see the result of such preaching, if preaching is the right word to use for such a matter-of-fact presentation of the facts about Jesus Christ, and the Scripture passages that explain them. The result was that the consciences of Peter's hearers were awakened. Peter did not, apparently, have to make any 'appeal' (though Paul on occasions certainly did (2 Corinthians 5: 20). Instead, the hearers themselves turned to Peter and the others and said, "What are we to do?" In other words, as we would say, the Holy Spirit had brought them to the place where they were convicted of their sin. But they had not yet come to the point of conversion, turning in sorrow and faith to Jesus Christ; for Peter had not yet come to that point.

□ The Follow-Up

Of course, Peter knows well how to do 'follow-up' work; he has a very practical answer to their question. They must 'repent': that, in the Bible, means far more than merely being sorry for sins committed—it means a total change of heart, rather what we mean by 'conversion'. But that is not all: they must have faith in Jesus Christ too—and they must show both their repentance and their faith by being baptised in the name of Jesus, the Christ. The aim of this whole response to God was so that their sins should be forgiven, and that they too should share in God's gift of the Holy Spirit. God's promises are there for them to claim and enjoy. This fact is true whether they are near to God (like the Jews) or far from Him (like the Gentiles, who have no Law). But, even at this stage, Peter is careful to explain to these new converts that this work of 'conversion' is something that God Himself has done, not something that they have done for themselves (all is in response to God's call).

☐ The Final Results

The final results were very wonderful: about three thousand 'accepted Christ', as we would say, and were baptised. The verses that follow (Acts 2: 42–47) describe their daily life after that; and it is an ideal picture of a church, but we may not stay to look at it now. Scripture itself, of course, reminds us that this was by no means all that Peter said. He, like any good preacher, 'pressed his case' and used 'many other words'. So we do not need to believe that we have in Acts either a full outline of his Pentecost sermon, or of his 'Follow-up' talk; but we believe it to be a fair summary of both.

☐ The Pattern

Here, then, we may say that we have an outline of the preaching of the apostles; and we can easily go through any of the other sermons in the early part of Acts, and make for ourselves similar outlines. We can then, if we are interested, compare these with the sermons of Paul later in the book. When these sermons are preached to Gentiles, there will be small differences on the surface, for Gentiles will not know as much of God's acts in history as the Jews will do. But they will know of God's activity in the world of nature around them; and they will know, through their conscience, something at least of God's Nature. More, even though they do not know Him, they will find in their hearts a longing to know and serve and worship Him. All of these things Paul will use as introductions; but the gospel will still be the same.

□ Spoken Gospels

Now, we know from the Acts of the Apostles that this sort of gospel was being preached everywhere. But the remarkable thing (to our way of thinking) was that as yet there were no Gospels, in the sense of the four written books that we now find when we open our New Testaments. That is what we meant when we said that the gospel comes before the Gospels, important though these are. But perhaps here somebody will be puzzled. We today could not possibly preach the gospel without the Gospels to quote from and to refer to; how then did Peter and the rest manage? The reason is simple and twofold: first, we did not say that they had no Bible; and second, there were in those days 'spoken Gospels' though as yet no written Gospels. We shall take these points one at a time.

You and I think it so strange that the early Christians had no Gospels to which they could refer when they preached the gospel to others, because that is the way in which we preach, and that is the way that we rightly look to God to bless. But this passage from Acts shows us that, in a sense, that is exactly what Peter and the rest did, in these early days, except that what they had and used was the Old Testament. They did not miss the Bible, because they had a Bible, although not, of course, as full as ours; and now that the Holy Spirit had opened their eyes, they saw how it spoke everywhere of Christ. In other words, they preached the gospel from the Bible; but they always used Old Testament texts.

☐ *Jesus and the Old Testament*

Of course, this use of the Old Testament is not only true of these early days of the preaching of the gospel in the Acts of the Apostles. In one sense, it was true long before, even when Jesus was upon earth: He constantly quoted the Old Testament to His disciples, to explain what He was going to do upon the Cross. So, in doing this, Peter and the rest were only doing what the Lord had taught them to do. In the other direction, it was true long afterwards. All through the rest of the New Testament, while the writers often refer to what Jesus said or did, and sometimes to what Paul or some other apostle said or did, they do not quote the Gospels. The Gospels, indeed, were probably not written until after most if not all of the Epistles. It is right that we put the four Gospels first in our copies of the New Testament, because, after all, they are fundamental. But this does not mean that, as books, they were written first, though of course the knowledge of Christ and His words and His doings contained in them was common knowledge to all the early Christians. That is why, in this little book the Epistles or Letters will be studied before the Gospels or Newscasts: and it also introduces us to the second reason why the early Christians did not as yet miss written Gospels.

□ *Living Gospels*

The reason is that they had what we might call 'living Gospels' walking round in their midst—indeed, evangelising them. Paul calls his converts 'living epistles' (2 Corinthians 3: 2). In a rather different sense, we may call the first generation of disciples 'living Gospels'. Every member of them must have had a tremendous fund of stories about Jesus, miracles that He had done, words that He had said, places that He had been—all of which they had seen and heard for themselves, and could tell at first hand to the converts. Who would want a book, when such men as these, who had been with Jesus from the time of John's baptism till Jesus' resurrection, and had met the risen Lord Jesus Himself face to face, could talk about Him? The time would come, soon enough, when this unique first generation would pass away; but, until then, there was no problem.

2 THE FIRST CHRISTIAN LETTERS

☐ *The Next Step*

Now, from the 'Gospel before the Gospels', we shall go at once to the Epistles. The reason for this is that most of them were written before our Gospels, although they were written by men that knew the gospel—indeed, had preached the gospel—and to men who knew the gospel—who, indeed, by hearing and obeying that gospel (Romans 6: 17) had been 'born again' by God's Spirit and had thus become members of Christ's Church. So, if we read the Epistles first, with the basic knowledge of the gospel in our mind and heart, we shall be reading them just as the early Christians did; and that may be a fresh and thrilling spiritual experience for some of us.

☐ *Letters to Christians*

What are the Epistles? If we remember the title of the translation of them by Canon J. B.

Phillips—*Letters to Young Churches*—it will at once convey the meaning of an old-fashioned word. But they are far more than ordinary letters, far more even than letters from great Christian pastors to their flock. Look at their length, for one thing: why, most of the New Testament epistles would be far longer than any ordinary letter, ancient or modern. Then, very few of them are addressed to individuals at all: perhaps the Epistles to Philemon, Timothy and Titus are the only ones coming under this heading, for it is not clear whether John, in his Epistles, is writing to individuals or to churches. Look at the subject matter as well. Normally, a letter deals with one or two points of business or news, of particular interest to the writer and the receiver of the letter. But these letters deal with the whole of Christian theology: what are we to make of that?

□ *Other Letters*

Can we find any parallels in the ancient world? Certainly we can find none in the modern world—unless an 'editorial article' in a Christian magazine, or a long letter to a newspaper is a parallel. Here the answer is puzzling, for it is both 'Yes' and 'No'. We have literally thousands of the letters that men wrote in Bible days—in Greek, the language of the New Testament, as well as Latin and Aramaic (the 'Hebrew' of Palestine). The sands of Egypt and the

19

caves of the desert of Palestine have been particularly rich in finds of this sort; but none are like our New Testament Letters in content whatever. Ours use the same style, the same greetings, but somehow the whole atmosphere is new.

□ New Wineskins

Are these 'Letters to Young Churches' an altogether new sort of letter, then? The answer seems to be "Yes": for we find no such letters before New Testament times, while after that, in the life and history of the Christian Church, they become common. Of course, such later letters do not claim to be 'inspired' in any way; but they are obviously modelled on the form of the New Testament Letters. Now, it is scarcely surprising that the gospel, which the Lord compared to 'new wine' (Matthew 9: 17), which could not be contained in the old leaky wine-skins of Judaism, should need fresh forms in literature to express itself—or rather, that God should create fresh forms, better able to express the gospel. We shall see, a little later, that exactly the same thing is true of the four books that we call 'The Gospels'. For there is nothing quite like a 'Gospel' book in the whole of the ancient world, whether inside or outside Judaism. Perhaps if we had more of the sort of letters that we know, from the New Testament and Jewish tradition, that Jewish Rabbis sent to scattered members of the Jewish 'family' overseas (see Acts 28: 21), we might have more parallels to the outward form of the New Testament Letters; but certainly we should have no parallel to their spirit—that was completely new.

□ Why Write Letters?

Why were such letters written? The reason is simple: to deal with the various practical problems that arose in the local churches, after the gospel had been preached to them, and after the Evangelist had moved on. In one sense, they are rather like the letters that a counselor at a boys' camp might send in the winter to some boy who had been converted at the last summer camp. He cannot now see the boy in person: even the boy's own memory of camp and counselor alike may be fading. But the counselor can still pray; he can still write and tell the boy that he is praying; and he can, on the basis of Scripture and his own spiritual experience, plus his understanding of that particular boy, try to deal with some, at least, of the spiritual problems that have arisen. That, for instance, is what Paul is doing in his Letters to Corinth. That is what makes the Letters so valuable to us: for some of their problems will be our problems too.

□ General Problems

But are all the Letters dealing with known problems of the local churches, planted so recently by Paul and the others? No, of course not all of them; but a good part of the Corinthian Letters, for instance, is taken up with problems which Paul knew only too well existed at Corinth. Indeed, a great part of First Corinthians is taken up with answering questions actually sent by the Corinthians to Paul. But, to return to the counselor—even if the boy, converted during the summer, has not written to him, telling him of problems, and asking him for advice, the counselor has still a very fair idea of the problems that will face him, both from his knowledge of boys in general, and of that boy in particular. He feels fairly safe, for instance, in supposing that there will be times when that boy will be tempted to doubt whether he is a Christian at all; or whether God can still love and forgive him, even when he is 'such a rotten Christian'. So he is safe to write on these subjects: and this is exactly what Paul does. For instance, he may never have been to Rome (Romans 1: 13), but he has a lot of friends there, and he knows that it will be a typical first-century (and first-generation) church. It is made up of both Jews and Gentiles? Good; but some problems of relationships will arise from this. So his understanding of Corinth and Ephesus and Antioch helps him to understand and sympathise with the Romans that he has never seen.

□ Special Problems

But does this mean that no church has special problems? By no means: Rome is right under the nose of imperial Caesar, for instance; special problems will rise from that. The Christian church at Jerusalem is under the shadow of the Temple (quite literally, until the Temple was burnt in A.D. 70; for the Christians seem to have met for worship in its colonnades). Special problems will rise from that. And, although we have no Letter to Jerusalem, we can form some idea of the problems from the 'Letter to the Hebrews', although it was probably written to 'overseas Jews' facing the same stresses and strains. But often these special problems will prove to be the special problems of some church today, even if in a slightly different form; and always the spiritual principles beneath will be the same.

□ Letters in Two Parts

But why then all the theology in the Epistles? We can see the point of an answer to a problem, known or guessed. But why burden these infant churches with complicated theology (which often seems even more complicated to us than to them, because we read it in old-fashioned English, while it came to them in the ordinary language of the shop or factory or office or farm)? Very often, when people are reading one of Paul's letters, they will divide it into two parts: 'Theological' (sometimes even called 'Theoretical') and 'Practical'. The first, they will dutifully read, because, after all, it is 'in the Bible'— like those long genealogies in Chronicles, or the lists of birds that one may not eat, to be found in Leviticus Now, most of us would not know a bald-headed eagle from a sparrow, apart from the size; and we have no desire to eat either. So, without thinking, we dismiss the section as irrelevant, and hurry on to something either more 'interesting' or 'practical'. (Both of these adjectives, by the way, are typical of our whole modern approach.) Most of us are tempted to treat the theology in Paul's Letters in the same way. But this is a great mistake: it is only in the light of the theology that the practical advice in the second half of the Letter makes sense, or indeed is possible. Paul is always saying "Because GOD is like this, you must be like that", or, more often, alas, "Because God is like *this*, you must *not* be like *that*."

□ *The Letters and Daily Life*

Are the Letters a development of the gospel? No; and a simple proof of this is that, by and large, the Letters were written by the same group of men that God would use to preserve and record the gospel in written form; but probably at a later date than most of the Letters. The Letters show us how the

24

truth of the gospel is to be worked out in daily life. Of course, not every possible situation is covered; but there are enough 'sample situations' covered in the New Testament to give us lines of guidance, so that we ourselves can work out, also with the Spirit's guidance, what we should do in the situations that confront us. In the theology of the Epistles, there is nothing that we cannot find 'in germ' in the Gospels—in some saying or deed of Jesus, or in some explanation given there. God wants children, not robots; and so, by studying these Letters, we grow in spiritual maturity, and ability to make wise spiritual decisions ourselves.

□ Growing Light

But surely the theology is more advanced than the Gospels? No, not really: it is only more systematically expressed. If the Gospels are like a garden full of flowers, then the Letters are like the keeper's cottage, just inside the gate—the walls covered with pictures of the flowers, along with their names, and plans of the botanical garden. Of course, we would not look in the Gospels for clear statements about the threefold Nature of God, as Father, Son, and Holy Spirit; for that, we must wait till the Epistles. But we find all the raw material for such a statement in the Gospels. And, when such statements are made in the Letters, it is in the knowledge of this fact, as well as in the light of the new and richer experience of Pentecost. As the Lord had promised (John 15: 26) it was only in the light of Pentecost, after their eyes had been opened by the Holy Spirit, that even the Lord's disciples understood the meaning of much that had gone before. So we must not talk of a 'Pauline' theology, if by that we mean anything other than a 'Christian' theology. Paul is but explaining the full implications of the facts about Christ that every Christian knows. He is telling other Christians the truths to which God's Spirit opened his eyes on the Damascus Road (Acts 9) and doubtless in the time spent in Arabia too (Galatians 1: 17).

□ *The Beginning of Christian Letters*
How did such letters begin? Well, even within the pages of the New Testament, we can see a letter of this sort being written by the apostles and elders of the Jerusalem church (Acts 15: 23–29) to their brethren among the non-Jews or Gentiles. We can see how a letter like this (a 'catholic' or 'general' letter, because not to any one place, though to a particular group) was widely spread and read. No doubt this is what happened later to Paul's Letters too, even if they were at first addressed to one particular church. Indeed, Paul himself seems to have suggested this sort of 'sharing of Letters' in Colossians 4:16. As for the material that we find in the Letters, Paul's

farewell speech to the Ephesian Elders at Miletus (Acts 20: 18–35) shows just the same concern to warn, and comfort, and strengthen the disciples. It was an easy passage from preaching this sort of message to writing it—especially when the imprisonment of Paul made any physical visit impossible (Ephesians 3:1).

□ Christian Rules

But are not some parts in the Epistles almost word-for-word the same? Yes, if you mean the list of instructions for behaviour within families, to be found in most of the Letters; or the list of qualifications for ministry in the Church, to be found in the 'Pastoral Epistles' (those to Timothy and Titus). But this is because every church was bound to need instruction like this: everywhere, there were husbands and wives, parents and children, masters and slaves. Furthermore, the Christian duties of such groups were perfectly clear; there could not be much variety in the treatment. Further, if any man is continually writing or preaching on the same subjects, he will tend to use the same words unconsciously—specially if he is an old man, as Paul describes himself as being in Philemon 9. There may well be another reason: we know that the Jews before the Christians drew up such 'House-Tables', as the Germans call them—lists of rules for right conduct within the home. As Paul and Peter and James and the rest were Jews, they may at least have been influenced by the order and plan of such 'lists', if not their content. Just as the Jews had used these 'lists' to teach Gentiles what was required of them, if they were to worship the True God, so Christian teachers would now draw up much more searching lists to show the Gentiles what was required of them if they were to work worthily of the calling of His Son, Jesus Christ (Ephesians 4: 1).

□ Filing Correspondence

But how were these Letters preserved? and how do they come to be in our 'New Testament' today? This is another question, and we must leave it until we discuss what is called the 'Canon' of the New Testament (roughly, its contents). At the moment, we are left with a number of Letters from Paul and other apostles, or at least first-century Christian leaders, sent either to particular churches (or even individuals) or else to wider groups. Naturally, these groups will read them with great interest— do not they deal with problems about which they have written to the apostles? At least, they will deal with situations and problems real to that Christian church. But why do they keep them? Most of us throw away our letters. And why should other churches read them? And, greatest question of all—why should we read them today, in a modern world so different from theirs?

□ Individual Pen-styles

But who wrote these Letters? We might of course say, "God the Holy Spirit", and we should be right. It was under the constraint and guidance of the Spirit that they were written: that is why they can still speak to our hearts today, as directly as they did to the hearts of those first-century Christians. But God has always been pleased to use human agents to work out His will in this world; and the Letters of the New Testament are no exception. Moreover, God does not obliterate the personality of His servants, when He fills them with His Spirit. Part of the fascination of Bible study is to see how God used the background and temperament of each apostle and writer, and how He trained and prepared each. We can even see the faults and shortcomings of each man, plainly recorded for us in Scripture. God does not paint idealised pictures of His servants—He paints them 'warts and all', as honest Oliver Cromwell would have it.

□ Who was Paul?

Many of the Letters of the New Testament begin, "Paul, an apostle of Jesus Christ". Who is this Paul? He is, like all the other writers of the New Testament, apart from Luke, a Jew; but he is an 'overseas Jew'. That means that in some respects his temperament is American, not English: he is at times a little impatient of the slow conservative ways

29

of James and the Jerusalem Jews. Stephen was another man of this sort, and with him Paul would have had a lot in common—had he not already joined in putting him to death? Saul, as his name was in the Synagogue, was the son of a well-to-do citizen of Tarsus, a flourishing commercial centre and university city on the south coast of Turkey. His father had somehow been granted Roman citizenship, a coveted privilege, for it gave security from arbitrary arrest and beatings, and an assurance of a fair trial, if it came to that. Tarsus was famous for its cloth, woven from the hair of the hardy little Cilician goats; it seems likely that Paul had been taught this trade from youth. (It is only fair to say that modern scholars are divided on the question as to whether he was a leather-worker or a cloth-worker, but to us the difference is not very great.)

□ *The Theological Student*

But how does a young cloth-worker become a letter-writer? The answer is that this manual labour was only a wise Jewish provision that every scholar should be able to support himself if necessary —and also so that he should not despise honest work. The 'absent-minded professor' of our jokes was utterly unknown to the Jews. Many of their greatest Rabbis were also distinguished for being sandal-makers or leather-workers. The Law, said they, was neither a 'spade to dig with' (something from which they could make money) nor yet a 'crown to wear on the head' (something to boast about). Perhaps this was why Paul was so ready to work later within Christianity as a 'voluntary pastor' (Acts 20: 34). Anyway, the young Saul came down to Jerusalem, where he received his training under Gamaliel, one of the most famous Rabbis or teachers of the day (Acts 22: 3). Again, some scholars think that the meaning of the Bible is that Saul actually grew up at Jerusalem: he certainly had a married sister living there in later days (Acts 23: 16). Either way, the point is not important: a brilliant young student, bigotedly devoted to Jewish traditions, young Saul grew up as a member of the Pharisees, the strictest and most rigorous group (Acts 23: 6). Small wonder that such a man was ringleader in opposition to the new 'heresy' of Christianity (Acts 8: 3).

□ *The New Beginning*

The conversion of Paul, in Acts 9: 1–22, explains all. From a bitter enemy of the Cross of Christ, Paul (he now uses his Roman name) becomes the devoted bondslave of the Lord (Romans 1: 1). Henceforth, to him, to live is Christ (Philippians 1:21), and he proves it by the way in which he 'burns out for God', blazing a trail for the gospel around the Mediterranean Sea. But always he writes with this background: he knows what it was to be a bitter enemy of the Cross; he knows what it is to be forgiven; who like he knows the blindness of Judaism? Who like he knows that the gospel can not only open the eyes but also change the entire nature? To him, the sharing in the death and resurrection of Christ was a peculiarly real experience: for, after the encounter with Christ on the Damascus Road, he had gone through three days of anguish and darkness in the house of Simon until Ananias had come with the glad news that brought light and joy and new life (Acts 9: 18).

☐ The Big Fisherman

What of the other Letter-writers? Peter we know well from the rest of the New Testament. If you are interested in Christian 'detective work', you may like to see how his First Letter reproduces many of the ideas found in Mark's Gospel (see the section on the Gospels for the link here) and also with those found in the early speeches of Acts (see the section on Christian history for some notes on this). Peter's First Letter is almost a 'Pastoral Epistle'; we can compare many points in the Letters to Timothy and Titus. By contrast, his Second Letter resembles, in places, the book of Revelation: see the section called 'Christian Prophecy'. This Second Letter is valuable for many reasons, not least for its assurance that such letters are written by eye-witnesses of Christ (1: 16–18), and for its helpful words on the nature of Scripture (1: 19–21).

□ Christian Circulars

Peter's Letters were not like Paul's, directed to one particular church and its problems: they seem to have been sent to the Jewish-Christian communities in North Turkey (where Paul seems to have never gone) that had been evangelised by the 'Apostle of the Circumcision', or 'Missionary to the Jews', as Peter was often called. Of course, they would have certain problems in common; and, while the churches are only names to us, to Peter, each name would doubtless bring up a picture of a group of people; for in the New Testament, the church is never a building, but a congregation. The Letter to the Hebrews is another 'circular' like this: we do not know who wrote it, for the Letter itself gives no hint— perhaps Apollos, or some other Jewish member of the apostolic circle. Certainly it too was written to Jews. Its whole argument is drawn from the Old Testament in a way which Jews would find peculiarly convincing. It shows the immense superiority, in every way, of Jesus to the priests and sacrifices of the Old Covenant. It is written to Jewish Christians somewhere or other who were in danger of leaving Christ and going back to the old ways. Wherever there are people, in Eastern or Western churches, who face this danger of going

c

back, this book will speak to them again. This in itself accounts for some of the stern warnings in the book: the danger is great.

☐ *Who Else?*

James, John, and Jude were others who wrote some of the New Testament letters. The John who wrote the letters is clearly the man who wrote the Gospel; we shall look at this in more detail under the section 'The Gospels', but if, as all early Christian tradition says, this was John the son of Zebedee, then we know a great deal about him. But, even without this, we could form a good idea of his gentle loving nature from the letters; and yet it is a nature that can be stern, when there is a question of some false teaching that will destroy the gospel (2 John 10). James writes a shrewd, practical Epistle. He must be the James who was Christ's brother, and the leading member of the church at Jerusalem, after the martyrdom of James the son of Zebedee (Acts 12: 2). He is greatly concerned, like any Jew, with correct behaviour—so much so, that at times, people have actually felt that his teaching ran counter to that of Paul. But of course this is not so: all that James is doing is balancing Paul's teaching on 'justification by faith', by showing us that this 'faith' must be warm and vital, not cold, dead, and only intellectual. Jude 1 merely tells us that he is the 'brother of James': if

34

the James in question was the brother of Christ, so was he. In his short letter, he reminds his Jewish–Christian hearers of the great lessons of the Old Testament, and tells them something of the great events that are to come. Most famous of all is the beautiful 'ascription' of glory to God that ends the book (Jude 24–25).

3 THE GOSPELS: CHRISTIAN 'NEWSCASTS'

☐ What are the Gospels?

What are the Gospels? Every Christian knows that they are Matthew, Mark, Luke, and John (probably with a subconscious instinct to add the line, "Bless the bed that I lie on"): but what exactly are these books? Supposing you really did meet a 'man from Mars', how would you tell him what they were? A good phrase from the New Testament that we might use is 'all that Jesus began both to do and to teach' (Acts 1: 1). But even when we say that, we realise that what we have is only a tiny fraction of His miracles and His teaching. In fact, John 21: 25 cheerfully tells us this—going on to tell us the obvious truth that the world itself would not hold the books, if every detail of the Lord's life was written down. But why in that case, do the Gospels repeat each other so much? Why does not each choose a totally different set of incidents, if there must be four of them? In any case, why should there be four and only four? Mark begins his Gospel (Mark 1: 1) by calling it bluntly 'the beginning of the Gospel of Jesus Christ': why did any others bother to write after that? Moreover, Luke 1: 1 equally cheerfully tells us that there were many other 'accounts' in existence before he wrote: why then did he write? And what has happened to these other 'Gospels'? These are some of the questions that we must try to answer gradually.

□ What is 'a Gospel'?

What does the title mean? If we want to understand the name 'Gospel', we must remember that although we may speak of the Gospel *of* John, the Bible always talks of the "gospel of Jesus Christ" (Mark 1: 1). It is true that Paul can speak of "my gospel", but, as he never wrote a 'Gospel', as far as we know, his meaning is evidently "the gospel that I preach" (Romans 2: 16). What the Bible talks of is 'The Gospel *according to* John', and that is something very different indeed. The Gospel, then, is something concerned from beginning to end with Jesus: and it is 'good news'. Probably the Greek word translated 'Gospel' in English began by meaning 'the reward given to the bearer of good news': but it soon became 'news' in general—and, for the Christian, in a revival of the old meaning at a deeper level,

37

God's good news of salvation for men, offered in the death of Jesus Christ upon the Cross.

□ The Town Crier

But is not the gospel something about which we preach sermons? No, not exactly, if we use Bible language: the gospel is either something that we 'newscast' (the Bible has a verb that means 'newscast good news'—it is our word 'evangelise' (Galatians 1: 8)) or else something that we 'herald', something that we announce by Town Crier, if we are old-fashioned, or broadcast over the amplifying system, if we are very up-to-date (1 Thessalonians 2: 9). In either case, it consists of a number of facts about Jesus Christ—what He did, what He said. The most important facts will be the story of His Cross and resurrection. Not only will the facts be told, but the meaning of those facts, as God showed it. When this is done, God's Spirit will use the 'word of the gospel' to speak to men's hearts: they will repent of their past lives, and believe in Jesus, and thus be 'saved' (Acts 16: 30) or 'born again' (1 Peter 1: 23) or receive 'everlasting life' (John 3: 16). All these, and many more, are of course just different words for the same experience; and all of this, the Bible is clear, is the work of the Holy Spirit (John 3: 5). Our responsibility is only to act as heralds of God, ambassadors for Christ (2 Corinthians 5: 20).

38

□ The Message

But what is the relation of this spoken gospel to our written Gospels? We have already seen, in Acts 2: 22, how Peter appeals to his own knowledge of the happenings of Jesus' life—a knowledge which is to some extent shared by his hearers—to evangelise; and we have seen the results in thousands turning to the Lord. By a little justifiable stretch of the imagination, we can see the same thing taking place throughout the whole New Testament world, wherever the first generation of Christians went preaching. Even Paul (who may or may not have seen some of the miracles of Jesus, and heard some of His teaching, even if he did not believe in Him—see 2 Corinthians 5: 16) can appeal quite confidently to the facts of His life. Why not? He had spent some time at Jerusalem, where he had inquired of Peter several matters, doubtless including this (Galatians 1: 18), and men like James, the Lord's brother, were his close friends. Obviously, there was no need among these particular Newscasters for a written Gospel—they preferred a spoken one.

□ Making the Record Permanent

What then made them change their minds? Why, after being so long content with a 'spoken Gospel', did they now want a 'written Gospel'? For this, there were two reasons: one is certain from the pages of the New Testament, while the second is a very likely guess. The problem did not become a real one, until that vital first Christian generation one by one began to die off. We see the change taking place as early as 1 Corinthians 15. Paul is discussing why he believes in the rising-again of Christ from the dead: to do this, he lists some of the many people who actually met Him after His resurrection. Most of these, he says, are still alive: then, almost sadly—for we are losing valuable witnesses— he says, "But some are fallen asleep" (1 Corinthians 15: 6). Of course, he would not say that they, any more than any other Christian, had 'died': we can only 'sleep' now, since the Lord's resurrection. But did the thought slip through his mind: how will it be if all the 'witnesses' have died, and the Lord has still not come again? As old age creeps on, he warns Timothy not to forget all that he has told him; and surely the Gospel-story is first and foremost among these. Furthermore, he warns Timothy that he, in his turn, must commit this knowledge to faithful men who will pass it on, even after him (2 Timothy 2: 2). But Peter is even more blunt: he tells the readers of his letter that he knows that he must soon 'break camp'; and so he is going to see that they have a permanent record of the things that he used to delight to tell them (2 Peter 1: 12–15). If we follow early Christian tradition, this 'permanent record' is none other than the book which we call the 'Gospel of Mark'.

□ *Early Paperbacks*

But was there anything before 'Gospels'? Did 'Gospels' just appear full-blown, or were there smaller, shorter books of the same sort first? This is one of those questions where we can never be sure of the answers, for the New Testament does not give one, and archaeology does not really help us. But, because the early Christians, even within the pages of the New Testament, quote so frequently from particular parts of the Old Testament, it does seem as if they had very early some sort of 'Pocket Companion for Christian Workers'—'Testimony Book' is the technical title—containing a number of passages from the Old Testament that could be used to prove to Jewish enquirers that Jesus really was the 'Messiah' for whom they waited. We probably have fragments of such books actually preserved among the sands of Egypt.

□ *Thumbnail Gospels*

But were there no other smaller 'Gospels'? The sort of 'Pocket Companions' that we have suggested would cover only a small part of the Gospel material, though a very important part (much of the early part of St. Matthew would roughly come under this heading, for instance). Here again, we do not know: but Luke's words in 1: 1–2 make quite clear that there had been numerous attempts to write

'Gospels' before his, and it is at least highly likely that some of them had not been full 'Gospels' in our sense of the word, but merely short collections of the sayings and doings of Jesus.

□ For Church Use

This brings us to the second of the two reasons why the Gospels were probably written down: they were not only to help the Church in witness, but also in worship. Christians did not only want handbooks to which they could turn, when wanting to confute or evangelise the heathen; they wanted something which they could read, when they met together on the Lord's Day, to remember Jesus their Lord—and in particular, to remember His death. When there were no longer aged disciples who could tell of these events firsthand, it was very natural that above all things they should desire written accounts of these things, resting on the authority and testimony of those who had known firsthand about Him. It may even be because they wanted such accounts to read at the Lord's Supper that all the Gospels give such attention to the last week of the Lord's life, centring on the Cross; but this is only guesswork. In any case, even apart from the Lord's Supper, every Christian would agree that the Cross is the centre of the Christian message, and thus fully deserves this attention.

□ Which Language?

What language were they first written in? This is a question that we do not have to ask about the Letters: they were written in Greek, just as we have them today. But it is very likely that some at least of these early 'Gospels' (though not the four that we now have) were originally written in Aramaic, the mother-tongue of Christ and His disciples in first-century Palestine. A Welshman or a Highlander may very well be able to speak, write, and read English: but he will probably prefer to chat to his fellow-countrymen in Welsh or Gaelic, as the case may be. We have many little traces of this left in our Gospels: *'ephphatha'* (Mark 7: 34), *'talitha cumi'* (Mark 5: 41) and so on. But this need not concern us, for our four 'Gospels' were undoubtedly first written in Greek.

□ New Wine for New Bottles

What about the form of the Gospels? That is one of the oddest things: just as Christians seem to have taken the old form of the Letter, and made a new thing of it, to express the new spiritual life that was seething all around them, so with the Gospels. There is nothing quite like the Gospels in the whole of the ancient world. The first century knew novels, and short stories, and biographies, and autobiographies: but a Gospel was none of them. It was not even an ordinary history, although the facts in it were all historical. It was just a Gospel, and that was all. It gave immense attention to one short week of the Lord's life, and never mentioned His boyhood (apart from one story in Luke 2: 41–51). The beginning of His life: yes—Matthew and Luke tell us of that. The end of His earthly life: yes, all tell of that. But in between, all that we have are a group of miracles and some of His teaching—especially in Matthew and John. This was something as distinctively Christian as the preached gospel itself: the new wine had found new bottles. So distinctively Christian was it that heretics (like the Gnostic 'Know-Alls') when they tried to write a Gospel (like the so-called 'Gospel of Thomas', found in the rubbish dumps of Upper Egypt) failed dismally. It just does not ring true, that is all: it is as unlike our Gospels as chalk is from cheese.

□ Stories about Mark

Have we any stories about how our Gospels came to be written? Yes, there are such stories, and quite early at that; but whether they are true or not, who can say? But first let us look at them, and then look at the Gospels themselves, and see whether they give us any clues as to the probable truth or not of such early accounts. Papias was bishop of a little town in Turkey about A.D. 130. He was old enough to remember the first generation of Christians, and he wrote thus (in a book called *Explanations of the Sayings of the Lord*): "Mark having been the interpreter of Peter, wrote down carefully, though not in order, all that he remembered, both words and deeds, of the Lord. For he had neither heard the Lord nor followed Him, but only at a later date, as I have already said, followed Peter. Peter arranged his instructions according to the needs and not as making an arrangement of the Lord's words. So Mark was not wrong to write down some things as he remembered them, for he took care to omit or falsify nothing which he had heard (from Peter)."

□ *And the meaning?*

What does Papias mean? This is all plain sailing: he says that Mark was Peter's 'interpreter' (either as explaining his sayings more fully, or simply as translating them into Greek for the benefit of non-Jewish people—for, of course, Peter's mother-tongue was Aramaic). Then, says Papias, Mark later (presumably, after Peter's death) wrote down carefully all that he could remember of Peter's teaching about Jesus: this is our Gospel of Mark. Papias informs us of two things, however, first, that Mark himself had not been a follower of Jesus, so that all his knowledge was second-hand. Secondly, he tells us that Peter selected and arranged his material according to his 'preaching needs', not necessarily according to the order in time. But, having said this, Papias reassures us by saying that he does not imply, in saying this, that Mark made any mistakes or was untrustworthy; on the contrary, he faithfully follows Peter's first-hand witness.

□ The Evidences of Peter's Contributions

Does this look likely, when we glance at Mark's Gospel? Yes, indeed, it does. The incidents mentioned in Mark's Gospel are just those that Peter would have known. The hardest words about Peter are in this Gospel; and it is very likely that, while other apostles might pass over unpleasant incidents in love, Peter himself, in his new-found humility, would remember them, and might insist on them being recorded by his young disciple. Furthermore, the way in which the gospel is presented in Mark's Gospel is exactly the way in which Peter, according to the independent witness of Luke, preaches the gospel in the opening chapters of Acts. Look this up for yourself: it will provide you with an interesting Bible study. Again, Mark's Gospel is very like the First Letter of Peter in many ways—a simple commentary will show you some of them.

□ Peter and Mark

But did Peter know a Mark? Yes, in 1 Peter 5: 13 Peter tells us of 'my son Mark': this is almost certainly not literal, but means that Mark is a beloved younger Christian. The same verse tells us that the two of them were together at 'Babylon', which seems to have been a sort of early Christian 'codeword' for Rome (presumably, to avoid getting into trouble with the secret police of the day). Now, from 2 Timothy 4: 11, we know that Paul asked Timothy to send young Mark to him at Rome: so it is almost certainly the John Mark of Acts 13: 5 etc. who is meant. The Jerusalem church met at his home (Acts 12: 12), and he may have been the 'young man' of Mark 14: 51.

□ And Matthew?

What does Papias say about Matthew's Gospel? He says, "Matthew put together in the Hebrew (i.e. Aramaic) language the Discourses (understand, 'the Discourses of Jesus'), and each one translated them as best he could." We must remember that, in those days, a word like 'Discourses' could be used in a wider sense: Papias does not mean that Matthew just wrote down something like a 'Sermon on the Mount', but that he composed some sort of a Gospel, in Aramaic, and for Jewish-Christians. This would quite clearly be Matthew the apostle; and so, as Mark's Gospel would rest on the eye-witness account of Peter, this Gospel would rest on the first-hand evidence of another apostle and follower of

Jesus, Matthew. When Papias says, "Each one translated them as best he could", he may either mean that, whenever Jewish Christians had to preach to Gentiles, they took this book and translated it as they went along (rather like a modern missionary might hold a Greek Testament in his hand, and yet preach from it in Chinese)—or he may mean that several different people afterwards translated this Aramaic Gospel of Matthew into Greek.

□ Matthew's Emphasis

What does Matthew's Gospel look like? Well, it is quite clearly written by a Jewish Christian and for Jewish Christians. It does contain a great amount of 'discourse', in the form of the Sermon on the Mount and the Parable. It has a great interest in the way in which Jesus, as King and Messiah, fulfilled all the prophecies of the Old Testament. But there the resemblance to what Papias says come to an end: for our Gospel is written in Greek, and does not show any obvious signs of being a translation, although it is thoroughly Hebraic in thought (and even, at times, in the poetic forms used—as in the Sermon on the Mount). Therefore it seems most reasonable to assume either that it is a later (Greek) Gospel written by Matthew after this early Aramaic one, or else that it is itself one of the 'translations' that Papias mentions. It would then be not *by* Matthew, but resting on his evidence—just as Mark's Gospel is not *by* Peter, but guaranteed by his testimony. If, as we have it, it was from the start written in Greek, this would account for the fact that it has no obvious signs of being a translation.

□ *And the Third Gospel?*

What about Luke's Gospel? Here we are on surer ground from the start, for, while Papias does not give us any help, the Bible itself gives more clues. Neither Mark's Gospel nor Matthew's Gospel say who wrote them (the titles at the top of the pages in our Bibles, are not in the Bible text itself, of course), but Luke's Gospel does, in a rather indirect way, as we shall see. Indeed, though we have no Papias to help us here, other early writers give us plenty of information about this Gospel. Irenaeus, a second-century bishop, tells us, 'Luke, the companion of Paul, put down in his book the Gospel which Paul preached.' Another early writer tells us that the two Gospels of Matthew and Mark already existed at the time; and that Luke's Gospel was written specially for Gentile converts to read. It also says that he was a Gentile and a doctor, as indeed do all early accounts. Whether he was indeed a man of Antioch, and whether the Gospel was written in Greece, and whether he really did die there, in a ripe old age, are details that we cannot check.

☐ *Any Clues?*

What does the Gospel itself suggest? The first few verses make clear that, when it was written, there were already, not just two, but 'many' Gospels in circulation. Perhaps some of these were different translations of Matthew's Aramaic 'Discourses of Jesus'. But, whatever they were, they have not survived—only Matthew and Mark have come down to us from this early period. Further, the writer tells us that, though he himself was not an eyewitness, he has been careful to rely on their evidence in writing his Gospel. Indeed, this is what he has done: for, apart from some other material, he has probably used both Mark and Matthew, and thus indirectly the evidence of two apostles and first-hand witnesses, Peter and Matthew. He addresses his Gospel to Theophilus, a man with a Gentile name, and apparently of high rank, to judge from the title that he is given (like the title 'Sir' nowadays). It seems as if this man is a Gentile convert under instruction, to judge from Luke 1: 3. More, the whole book shows a great interest in the Lord's dealings with Gentiles (as, incidentally, it does in His dealings with sinners and women). A lot of argument has raged around the question as to whether this is a doctor's Gospel: what do you think? We may not be competent to judge as to whether or not he uses medical language, but at least we can see his medical interest in the healing miracles of Jesus: that seems plain.

50

But how does all this link the Gospel with Luke? True, the name does not appear directly in the Gospel (any more than Mark's name does in his Gospel, nor Matthew's nor John's in the other two), but it seems certain from Acts 1: 1 that the author of Luke's Gospel was also the writer of Acts. (We shall think more of this when we come to the section on Christian history later.) But we still have not proved them both by Luke: no, and we cannot prove it, for not even Acts contains Luke's name as author. But we know that Luke was a travel-companion of Paul (2 Timothy 4: 11), and Paul himself tells us that Luke was a doctor (Colossians 4: 14). Enough now to say that, if Luke the doctor wrote Acts (and there is every reason to believe that he did) then Luke the doctor wrote the Gospel too. Perhaps his doctor's fondness for 'case-histories' helps him to record with carefulness those early stories about the birth and boyhood of Christ not contained in other Gospels; and his quick Gentile sympathies prompt him to record the parables like the Lost Sheep, the Lost Coin, and the Lost Son, only found in his Gospel. As a Gentile, too, he is careful to explain Jewish words and customs; again, as a Gentile, he finds them quaint and records them, where a Jew might pass over them as familiar. Luke writes with all the artistry of the first-century Greek; he is an educated man, a 'professional man', with gifts consecrated to his Lord.

□ Stereoscopic Vision

What do we mean by 'the Synoptic Gospels'? Roughly, what we mean is: Matthew, Mark, and Luke, because they give a 'synoptic' (we would say 'stereoscopic') picture of Jesus. These three Gospels run, approximately again, along similar lines, although Papias has warned us that Peter does not stick strictly to a time-order. Yet, by and large, we have three parallel accounts of the life and ministry of Jesus, from His birth to the Cross and resurrection. Some Gospels go further than others. Some Gospels are fuller than others. Each overlaps the others to some extent. Each contains some material that is not in the other two. But, compared with John, they do fall together as a group: why John is a little different, we shall see below.

□ The Relationship of Matthew, Mark and Luke

What is meant by 'the Synoptic Problem'? All that is meant is the question of the exact relationship of Matthew, Mark, and Luke—how they came into being, which borrowed from which, and so on. This is all very interesting, but it is really a 'specialist's question', and need not concern us directly if we are content, as the early Church was, to accept each Gospel in turn as God's gift to us, and bringing its own special message and insights to our hearts, while all containing the common story of

Jesus. Most Protestant scholars, for example, believe that Matthew and Luke both used Mark. Many Roman Catholic scholars believe that Mark and Luke both used Matthew. Perhaps the true answer is that all alike used a common bódy of material that told of Jesus' words and deeds.

□ The Fourth Gospel

What about the Gospel according to John? Quite clearly, this is different from the other three 'Synoptic' Gospels: why is this? As usual, there are plenty of stories in the early Church to explain this difference, which they saw just as clearly. Irenaeus tells us two things: one, that this Gospel was written after Matthew, Mark, and Luke; two, that it was written by John the Apostle, while he was living at Ephesus. Apparently, Papias also reported this, although his work is now lost; other early fathers tell us that it was written after the book of Revelation. Clement of Alexandria (about the end of the second century) tells us that John's Gospel was specially written as a 'spiritual' Gospel, since John felt that the outward life of Jesus had been sufficiently treated in the other three Gospels. So much for the early evidence: now let us look at the Gospel itself.

□ All is anonymous

What does the Gospel itself claim? Once again, its title is 'the Gospel according to

John', but that might only mean that John's authority, as an eye-witness, is behind it—just as no doubt Peter's authority is behind Mark, and Matthew's behind the Gospel according to Matthew. But even this title is not part of the Bible itself; so we are not much further on. Within the Gospel, all is anonymous—perhaps for reasons of safety in persecution.

□ Indirect Clues to Authorship

Are there any indirect clues? Yes: the Gospel contains several carefully veiled references to the disciple whom Jesus loved: from the context, this is clearly John. Now, in the ancient Jewish world, to refer to oneself indirectly in the third person like this was good manners; but the clue is still uncertain. Furthermore, the writer of this Gospel knows much of the 'inner life' of Jesus, in a way that implies particular intimacy and friendship: and the Bible is clear that only Peter, James, and John enjoyed this privilege. In addition, John 21: 24 identifies this 'beloved disciple' with the one who not only bore first-hand witness to the deeds and words of Jesus, but also wrote them down; indeed, John 21: 25 contains the only 'first-person' reference in the book. Lastly, it seems quite clear that the same person wrote both the Gospel and the Letters; and in I John 1: 1-3, the author claims to have been an eye-witness of the life and ministry of Jesus Christ. No name is given in the

54

Letters (other than the title 'the Elder') but early tradition is unanimous that the writer was John the apostle.

□ John's Style

But what about the style of John's Gospel? That is one of the first things that strikes us: the other three Gospels (especially perhaps Mark) seem blunt and straightforward and somehow businesslike; John, by contrast, seems dreamy and meditative. If Mark's Gospel were written by a Martha, then John's Gospel would have been written by a Mary: that is the impression left on our minds—and it may well contain a deep truth. The real question that puzzled scholars asked was: did Jesus really teach and speak like that? And, if He did, why does it not appear in the other Gospels? 'Liberal' scholars solved the question by saying bluntly that Jesus never spoke like that. This, they said, was all John's style, if not John's material: Jesus actually taught and spoke in the style of the other Gospels. More, they said that this style of John showed that the Gospel was very late, and much influenced by Greek thought. Of course, 'Conservative' scholars were not happy with this: but what was the answer?

□ Christ's Teaching Style

The answer lies, firstly, in saying that, even in the other Gospels, Jesus uses, not only one style, but many—ranging from the poetic forms on the Sermon on the Mount to the pithy proverbs that He quotes elsewhere. Moreover, there is one famous passage, occurring in two earlier Gospels, where Jesus uses exactly the style and thought found in John: it is the passage beginning in Matthew 11: 25 and Luke 10: 21. Look it up for yourself. If the average Christian were asked from what Gospel this verse came, nine out of ten would say 'John' without hesitation. So the other Gospels, too, bear witness that this was one of the 'teaching styles' of Jesus. It seems from Matthew and Luke as well as John that this was His style in prayer and meditation, rather than in public preaching. John's very closeness to his Lord may account for the fact that he has recorded more of His 'inner moments'. Indeed, it may well be that his Master's style has influenced that of John; but this is of course mere guesswork.

□ *Names and Places*

Have we any other reasons to trust John's Gospel? Yes: one of the contributions of modern Biblical archaeology has been to show us, for instance, that the numerous names of indi-individuals preserved in John (Mary, Martha, Lazarus, for example) were the very names common in first-century Judaism. It has also showed us that whoever wrote this Gospel had a detailed knowledge of Jerusalem as it existed before the Romans utterly destroyed it in A.D. 70, when many of the old familiar landmarks went for ever (as many parts of London did in air-raids, for instance). When John talks about Gabbatha, or the Pavement, in 19: 13, it is a reference that no early Christians could understand. We, thanks to archaeologists who have cleared away, from on top, all the rubble left by the siege, can see and understand. Moreover, since the discovery a few years ago of a 'cache' of old manuscripts, roughly dating from the time of Christ, on the shores of the Dead Sea (and hence called the 'Dead Sea Scrolls'), we have many parallels to the style, language, and choice of words in John's Gospel. Although the Scrolls are in Hebrew, and the Gospel in Greek, yet they show us that the thought of the Gospel is neither late nor Greek, but thoroughly Jewish and first-century at that.

□ *A Christian Supplement*

But what of the contents of John? We might not find it any problem if it was just the style that was different; but it does seem as if the contents are different too—so much so that it is hard to fit John into a 'Gospel Harmony', while it is fairly easy to work in the others. The answer to this probably lies in the early tradition of the Christians: which said that this was written after the other Gospels, and also written to give us a 'spiritual' Gospel. By this last, they meant that John deliberately wrote his Gospel to give us the 'inner story' which he, almost alone among the apostles, knew. If he does not refer to something which is told in all the other Gospels, it does not mean that he was ignorant of it, still less that he did not believe in it. (Actually, he often refers to such happenings in an oblique way—see any commentary on John, for examples.) It simply means that he feels that this incident has already been sufficiently recorded; therefore he either passes it over in silence, or interprets its inner meaning, or gently corrects some possible misunderstanding by us of the Synoptic account, by adding a few more details. The suggestion made above that, in John's Gospel, we have the 'meditative style' of Jesus would agree both with the witness of the early Church, and the evidence of the Gospel itself, if we take this view.

4 THE FIRST CHRISTIAN HISTORY

□ Christian History Begins

When we say 'Christian History' we mean the Book of Acts—or the Acts of the Apostles, to give it its usual full name. This does not mean that the Gospels are not historical, or the Epistles for that matter; but Acts is a different kind of book from the others, that is all. We might almost have called it the first 'Church History' ever written, for it sets out to give us a connected account of how the gospel spread from Jerusalem to Rome. There are stops, either because the history had then been brought up-to-date at the time of writing, or because the writer felt that he had shown all that he wanted to show. Like all histories, ancient and modern, the author does not try to record every fact: he chooses those that he thinks most important for his purpose. Nor does he always give us exact dates for the different events; perhaps he did not always know the exact date, or perhaps he just was not interested. But nevertheless the writer is the first great Christian historian of all time.

□ The First Christian Historian

Who wrote Acts? This is a question that we have glanced at before, but we must tackle it more seriously now. As to the belief of the early Church, there is no doubt: with one voice, the early Christians said that Acts was the work of Luke, the Gentile doctor, and companion of Paul on at least some of his missionary journeys. Now, the interesting thing is that, as neither Acts nor the Gospel mentions the name of an author (though both are clearly by the same hand), this must be independent evidence. Furthermore, there is no reason why the early Christians should make up a story like this (even if we should consider them capable of doing such a thing) for Luke was not an important person, either in the New Testament or outside it. In fact, there was no reason at all why his name should be attached to these books, unless he really had something to do with them.

□ A Christian's Guide to History

But what does Acts itself say? Very little, as usual: but it does say that both Gospel and Acts were written and planned as part of an early 'Christian's Guide' Series. The Gospel was to deal with all the doings and teachings of Jesus, until His resurrection and ascension; Acts was to be the sequel, the next instalment, of the serial story (Acts 1: 1–2). Both books are dedicated to the same convert, Theophilus, who seems to be an influential non-Jew. But, apart altogether from the very similar introductions to Gospel and Acts, if the two are by the same man, we would expect the wording and style to be the same: and this is the case. Furthermore, in the Acts, there is a whole series of passages that are called the 'We-passages', because the author stops saying 'Paul' and instead says 'We' (see Acts 16: 11). Now, as these are exactly the same style as the rest of the book, this must mean that, for that particular part of Paul's journeys, the author of the book travelled with Paul. That narrows the circle down still further: for we know most of Paul's travel-companions by name—and Luke was one of them (Colossians 4: 14). Also, it cannot be any of the travel-companions mentioned by name in the 'we-passages', or he would have said 'I'. That narrows the circle a great deal further. Indeed, to judge from the New Testament, only Luke, Demas, and Crescens are likely candidates; and we have seen that all early Christians are agreed that it was Luke.

□ *You Can Identify a Doctor*

Can we tell that the book of Acts was written by a doctor? Here again, opinions vary:

it will certainly make a very interesting Bible study for you to go through Acts, and find out what you think. Scholars have argued backward and forward on the question as to whether there is medical language in the book or not. Most of them feel that, if so, there is not enough to *prove* that the author was a doctor, though there is enough to make it highly likely. This is the sort of question that is beyond most of us; but we can see how the author likes to describe illnesses and cures in detail (Acts 3: 7 and 9: 18, for instance). If it is indeed by a doctor, then of course it must be by Luke; we know of no other in the early Christian circle—which was not as yet very large, and still consisted mostly of humble folk.

☐ Jew or Gentile?

Can we tell that it was written by a non-Jew? Not for sure, of course, but we can make a good guess. To begin with, the book is addressed to a non-Jew, Sir Theophilus, a Roman 'knight'. We are not to think of him as some Sir Lancelot in shining armour, but perhaps some wealthy Roman 'civil servant'—Sir Bill Bloggs, in fact. Then there is the excellent Greek in which the book is written: further, there is the detailed knowledge of the Roman world of the first century contained in it. Luke is, like any Greek, intensely interested in 'local colour', and reproduces it very faithfully. Look at the way he has captured exactly the Jewish atmosphere of the Jerusalem church, for instance, in Acts 1–7, just as he did in the opening chapters of his Gospel. If he uses an Aramaic word, he will explain it for his fellow-Gentiles (Acts 1:19). But perhaps the strongest argument that the book is written not only by but for Gentiles is drawn from the fact that it was written at all: let us then ask a question.

□ Trial by Jury

Why was Acts written? We have said that it was a sequel to Luke's Gospel, that is plain from 1:1. But why have such a sequel at all? After all, Matthew and Mark have no sequel, unless it be the Epistles. Some have suggested that Acts was written as an 'apology' for Paul—a book that could be produced at his trial at Rome, to prove that Paul was guiltless of all the charges of sedition brought against him by the jealous Jews. Those who say this usually point to the way in which Luke, in Acts, is careful to record how Roman officials protected Paul in every place. This shows that they, at least, had believed in his innocence; this might influence Paul's present judges. That, they say, is why the book ends so suddenly: it brings the story of Paul right up to his trial—probably the first trial, at which he seems to have been acquitted (2 Timothy 4: 17). This suggestion is interesting, but pure guesswork. Another suggestion, at least as likely, is that here we have the story of how the Gospel travelled from Jewish Jerusalem to Gentile Rome, the capital of the known world in those days. Now this was a story which would grip any Gentile Christian; and it is most likely to have been written by a Gentile for them to read. True, an 'overseas' Jew like Paul could have written a book like this; but hardly one of the Jerusalem group. Even though Luke wrote it, we can be sure that Paul approved— unless, as some say, he had been already martyred. If he had, that might account for the abrupt ending of the book.

□ *The Speeches*

What are the 'speeches' in Acts? In several places in Acts, but especially in chapters 1–7, we have quite long speeches, by Peter, Stephen, and others. In the later chapters, we have one by James and several by Paul. As we have said when we were talking about 'the Gospel before the Gospels', these are very valuable, because they show us what the Christian Church believed and preached before there were any written Gospels. Of course, Luke does not give us the whole of what was said on each occasion; but he gives us enough of an outline to show us the line that the speaker took, and the beliefs that he held. As a matter of fact, the speeches do much more than this: they give us a very fair idea of the characteristics of the speaker.

□ Who Made the Speeches?

But how do we know that Luke did not make them up? That is a question that may puzzle some people. After all, one of the famous Greek historians tells us quite calmly that *he* made up speeches like this. Of course, Thucydides did not do this to deceive anybody; he tells us quite frankly —thus showing us that, to him, speeches were just like the 'learned notes' that we find at the back of modern books. But Luke's speeches are not like that: when we compare Peter's speeches with Mark's Gospel and First Peter, we find the same sort of approach. When we look at Paul's 'outline sermons' in Acts 13 and 17, we find just the approach that we also find in Paul's Letters to the churches. But Luke himself could not possibly have known all that every leader thought and taught; Paul he did know well, but not the leaders of the Jerusalem church. He could not have made up these speeches himself, he did not have the material: so what we must have here is faithful reporting.

□ A Popular Book

One of the most interesting things about Acts is that it is one of the few books of the

Bible that is read widely even by people with no special Christian interests. If people want to find out about sailing methods in the ancient world, they turn to Acts 27, the shipwreck—though the scholars tell us that there are more signs of the doctor than the sailor in this passage. If they want to find out details about the geography and history of the first-century Roman world, they turn to the other chapters of Acts. Luke delights to give us, for instance, the special title of local officials in the different places: it is as though he told us which cities had Aldermen and which had Councillors. Any commentary on Acts will give examples: two instances are 'Asiarchs' in Acts 19: 31 (A.S.V.) and 'chief man' of Malta in Acts 28: 7. Directions, distances, names, titles, customs—Luke is a real mine of information on these matters.

□ Why Read 'Acts'?

What is the chief Christian value of Acts? It would be hard to single out its 'chief' value, for it teaches us so much. Some have felt that its chief value was the teaching about the coming and work of the Holy Spirit, and so they have suggested that a better title for the book would be 'The Acts of the Holy Spirit'. Others see its greatest value as being its evidence about the early Church—how it witnessed, how it worshipped, how it was governed, how it grew. Still others will see its chief value in the 'background' that it gives for the understanding of Paul's letters and the rest of the New Testament. But, from whatever angle, its value is inestimable.

5 CHRISTIAN PROPHECY

□ Christian Prophecy

What do we mean by 'Christian Prophecy'? It is simply an attempt to get a title that will cover the book of Revelation (as well as parts of other books in the New Testament) and, at the same time, show its link with the Old Testament. In a sense, every part of the New Testament may be said to correspond with one part of the Old. If the Gospel is roughly parallel to the Law, then the Epistles are roughly equivalent to the Prophets —for in both, the principles already revealed are being explained in terms of the daily life of God's people. Corresponding to the history of God's people in the Old Testament, we have the history of the new people of God in the New Testament; and like the books that are called 'apocalyptic' in the Old Testament, we have the book of Revelation in the New.

□ Drawing Back the Veil

What do we mean by 'apocalyptic'? It is just the Greek word for 'unveiling'; and 'revelation' is the same word in its Latin dress. In this type of book (like Daniel, for example) God 'unveils' something of His plans and purposes for man. Sometimes, this is to show the true meaning of His present dealing with His saints; more often, it is to explain their present position and suffering by pointing to the future. So Biblical 'apocalypse' is usually, though not always, concerned with the future, whether near or immediate.

□ But Why?

That shows us the purpose of Apocalyptic. It is never given to us so that we can become amateur prophets ourselves, and forecast future world events. Indeed, it seems to be deliberately given to us in such general terms that we cannot do this—as though God Himself were discouraging us from such activity. Even the Lord Himself, Who was well read in all the Old Testament prophets, said that He did not know of the exact time of His own return to this earth (Matthew 24: 36): that was a secret known only to the Father. But that He is coming again is something clearly stated in prophecy. These truths are revealed so that we may hold fast, and so that we may live lives, here and now, that are well-pleasing to God (Matthew 24: 42).

□ Trumpets or Rockets?

What of the language of Apocalypse? Naturally, New Testament Apocalypse takes over much of the style and language of Old Testament Apocalypse. We have one style for telegrams ('CHANGE OF PLAN RETURN DELAYED LETTER FOLLOWS', for example) which we would never think of using in our ordinary letters. Also, like any other New Testament writer, the writer of the Revelation was steeped in the Old Testament. Similarly, every first-century Jew was—just like our grandparents were steeped in the English of the Authorised Version of the Bible. That is why, at first sight, some of the symbols and pictures used in the book of Revelation seem strange to us today—horses of various colours, and trumpets blowing, and basins being tipped out over the earth, and so on. But to any reader of the Old Testament, these will be old familiar symbols, and he will be reassured, not puzzled by them. True, if God had revealed it in our day, He might have used jet-planes and spaceships and rockets as symbols: but in a few hundred years, even these would have read just as strangely.

□ Spiritual Algebra

What do we mean by 'symbols' and 'pictures'? does that mean that the book of Revelation is not 'real', not 'fact'? No: it does not mean that. When we use 'mathematical symbols' in algebra or some engineering formula, it does not mean that the statement is not true, or that the formula will not work. As a matter of fact, it means the very opposite: it means that this is something that is always true, and will always work. Now, the difference here is that we are not dealing with mathematical symbols, but with spiritual symbols. What we mean is that God is using pictures drawn from this physical world of ours to describe great realities in the spiritual world. The spiritual reality may and will be far greater than our understanding of it here and now —for Paul warns us that, while in this world, we can only know in part (1 Corinthians 13: 9)—but, as this is the way that God has chosen to reveal His truth to us, we know that we shall not be misled if we think of the spiritual reality in this way.

□ Foretelling and Forthtelling

Is this the only sort of 'New Testament prophecy'? No: in the New Testament (and particularly in Paul) 'prophecy' seems to have two distinct meanings. At least, it has two meanings which seem distinct to us, but they cannot have seemed distinct to the writers of the Bible, or else they would have used two words not one. The first meaning is 'prophecy' in the sense of 'foretelling the future'. Some New Testament saints had this gift from God, as some Old Testament saints had had it before them. A good example is Agabus, who, in Acts 11: 28, foretold a great famine that was to take place. The church of Antioch took very practical steps as a result, and it was well that they did: for such a famine did actually come. Not only so, but in Acts 21: 11, he clearly foretells, both by acts and word, that Paul will be imprisoned at Jerusalem, But, as in 1 Corinthians 14: 6, when Paul uses the word 'prophecy' in his epistles, he seems more often to refer to what we would now call 'Biblical exegesis' or even 'Biblical preaching' The word means the declaration of God's mind and God's plans, under the influence of the Holy Spirit. This type of 'prophecy' has of course remained with the Church, though men like Agabus seem to have disappeared with New Testament days. After all, even in the Old Testament, it has often been pointed out that the prophets are not only 'foretellers'—they are also 'forthtellers' of God's mind.

□ *Where else?*

What other parts of the New Testament are 'Christian prophecy'? Of course, if we take

'Christian prophecy' in this wider sense, we could say that nearly all of the New Testament came under this heading. But even in the narrower sense, we could give 1 Thessalonians 4: 15-17, 2 Thessalonians 2: 1-12, 1 Corinthians 15: 20-28, and 2 Peter 3: 10-13 as obvious instances from the Letters. In the Gospels, there is one famous passage which is often called 'the Little Apocalypse', because it is so similar to the book of Revelation; it is found in Mark 13 and Luke 17. The most important thing about this last passage is that it shows us that the Lord Jesus Himself thought about the future in these terms; otherwise, we might just think that it was a Jewish 'hangover', something that we need not bother about. These other passages all help us to understand Revelation better: read them for yourself, and compare their messages.

☐ Who Drew the Veil?

Who wrote the Book of Revelation? Like the Book of Hebrews, we really do not know; nor indeed is it a very important question. The book itself says that it was written by a John, who was a prophet. He was at the time in Patmos, a little island in the east of the Mediterranean Sea, famed for stone-quarries, and used by the Roman government as a penal settlement for prisoners. But he does not say that he was an apostle, nor does he say that he was the brother of James; so we cannot be sure whether he was the 'son of Zebedee' or not. If he *was* (as early tradition claims) that would explain many interesting links between Revelation and the Gospel of John. Even if he was not John the Evangelist, the author was clearly one closely in touch with the Apostolic circle, and probably belonged to the first Christian generation himself.

☐ A Book for Concentration Camp

When was it written? Again, the exact date is not very important; but it will help to understand its message if we can understand the sort of circumstances amid which it was produced. It may have been written some time at the end of Nero's reign, perhaps about A.D. 68; or else under the Emperor Domitian, about A.D. 95. The point is that both of these were times of bitter State persecution for the Christian Church. This may be hard for people living in modern Britain or America to understand; but for those of us who live in other parts of the world, where the government is not 'Christian', it is easier to grasp. For some of our brethren, who live in 'totalitarian' countries, this is a present reality and daily experience. Naturally, for them the Book of Revelation 'comes alive' in a way that it does not for us. In Europe, some of the best commentaries on Revelation have been produced in 'concentration camps'. That is why the attitude to the state, typified by the Roman Emperor, seems so different in, say, Paul's Letters, and the Book of Revelation. In Paul's day, the state had still been the protector of the Christians against violence, as we saw from the book of Acts; now, the state has become a persecuting monster, drunk with the blood of Christians.

□ The Letters to the Churches

How is the book made up? After an introductory account of John's vision, it goes on to the Letters to the churches, in Revelation 2–3. These, though brief, are very like Paul's Letters in many ways: they show the same knowledge of local conditions, and the same pastoral concern. The main difference is that they are also 'prophecy', in that they foretell what the Lord will do to these various churches in years to come. Perhaps Paul's farewell speech to the Ephesian Elders in Acts 20 is his nearest approach to this: for in it, he tells them what God has revealed to him concerning their future and his. This is the part of Revelation that most of us know best, and it is most immediately applicable to the life and work of our own local churches; but it is a great pity if we neglect the great visions that fill the rest of the volume. Perhaps we had better treat them in a paragraph of their own.

□ The Visions of Revelation

What about the visions of Revelation? If we attempt to study them in detail, we may get confused, or lost in small points. Revelation is really like a great masterpiece of painting: first we need to stand back, and appreciate the whole; then we can come closer, and see how each part fits into that whole. All that we can attempt to do here is to give an 'approach', a broad outline, as it were. If we think of the visions as scenes in a great play, or as movements in a musical composition, we shall not go far wrong. As in a play, there are often tranquil 'intervals' between the scenes, to relieve the tension, or to show us some other relevant facts 'behind the scenes'. So we have the Vision of the Seven Seals; then that of the Seven Trumpets; then that of the Seven Bowls; then that of the Beast with Seven Heads; then the great battle—and final triumph of God (we have had glimpses of this before, in earlier quiet 'interludes'). After this comes the fruit of victory—the New Jerusalem—and all is peace at last.

□ Their Interpretation

But how do we interpret the visions? Even if the lesson of the final triumph of God and His Christ is clear, how do we interpret the details? Do any of these pictures stand for the happenings of our day? And, if not, what do they stand for? Here

Christians have never been quite agreed, so we do well not to be too dogmatic about our own views. One group of Christians see in it a continuous historical account of relations between the world and the Church, until the end of time; but, as they are not agreed at what point we are now standing, that is not much practical help for us today. Others see it all as describing what will happen just before the Lord returns again; that again is very interesting, but it is hard to see what it had to do either with first-century Christians or has to do with us (apart from confirming this great hope in our hearts, of course). Perhaps one could combine these views, and say that it may mirror to some degree the sufferings through which the Church was passing under Nero or Domitian; it describes in an illustrative sense what the Church will always suffer at the hand of the world; and it assures us of the final triumph of God in history, including the last judgment and the establishment of the eternal reign of God. No doubt, when the final triumph of God comes, as we look back, we shall see how all of these, and far more, have been very wonderfully fulfilled and realised.

□ Their Practical Value

The practical value for us has already been mentioned. Of course, if we are a church at the moment suffering terrible persecution at the hands of a heathen state, it has a very special message for us. But even if we are not yet in that position, Revelation is a very precious book; for all of us are conscious of the oppression of sin, and of a world implacably arrayed against God, a world whose power seems as great as its hate. Yet here is the peep 'behind the scenes': all is not lost—far from it. The end is sure from the very beginning, all that we have to do is to 'hold fast'. Not only so, but, as elsewhere in the New Testament, the hope of the Second Coming of Christ becomes not only the great comfort in our despair, but also a powerful incentive to present holy living. He who reads the Book of Revelation thus will never be tempted to think of it as irrelevant in any age. But there is, of course, far more in Revelation than that: read it for yourself, and see.

6 FORMING THE CHRISTIAN LIBRARY

□ The Pocket Library

We have seen how 'the books' came into being—but what of 'the Book', for this is of course what 'the Bible' means? Why was it that these books were selected out of what seems to have been a much larger number, and why did they survive? And how did they come to be differentiated from other books? How, for instance, did they come to be placed with, and even above, the books of the Old Testament, which the infant Church had already, as part of its legacy from Judaism? We must remember that the reasons may be slightly different in the case of various parts of the New Testament; but there are certainly broad general principles that we can see. Moreover, apart from a few hints in the New Testament itself, we must use guesswork for the early period. By the time, a few centuries later, we come to what is called 'the formation of the Canon', we have more information; but, by then, the question is virtually settled. Already, by then, there is a 'New Testament' in existence. It is just a question of recognising its existence, and defining its exact limits.

□ A Series by Paul

Let us start with the Pauline Epistles, since these probably came first in any case. We know that one early collection at least, which became one of the bases for our New Testament, was a collection of thirteen Letters of Paul. Now, how did this come about? We can only guess: but it seems very natural that Paul's Letters to a particular church should be treasured by that church, and read over again and again at meetings for worship. If, as usual, a Letter dealt with one of the constant and continual problems of that church, it was the more likely. We can presume that, after Paul's martyrdom, they would value these letters even more. Now the voice that they had loved was silent for evermore, not merely absent for a time. Other letters from venerated church leaders were likewise preserved in later days; but, completely unlike these later letters, Paul claimed to be inspired when he wrote—these were no ordinary letters. This in itself would secure the more careful preservation.

□ Some Lost Titles

But were all Paul's Letters preserved? No, by no means; and while the Christian sees this as due to the overruling of God, he may still ask what the reasons were. For example, we know from the New Testament that Paul wrote at least three (and maybe more) letters to Corinth (e.g. 2 Corinthians 2: 3-4, ,which obviously cannot refer to our 1 Corinthians). Only two of these survive. We know that he wrote one to the Laodiceans (Colossians 4: 16): but this too is lost. It seems reasonable to assume that he wrote letters to others of the churches that he founded; but, if so, these have left no trace. Perhaps the answer is that a church which flourished and grew (like Rome—or Corinth, for all its troubles) would be likely to preserve these letters; while a weak church like Laodicea (Revelation 3: 15) might be expected to lose all trace of them, with its general abandonment of spiritual values. Rome, Greece, Asia Minor: these are the three great areas where we know of Paul's sustained missionary activity; and it is just to these three areas that the surviving Letters are addressed. Perhaps it was only in these three areas that they were read and treasured, before finally being brought together.

□ *Reading Other People's Letters*

But what of the steps in between? This is easy. As we have seen in the section under 'Christian Letters', Paul himself (no doubt to save himself endless repetition of similar material) asked local churches to share the letters that they got from him, and thus to pass on the news (Colossians 4: 16). Of course, if a letter was 'catholic' (that is 'general', addressed to the Christian community at large, not just one particular church) this was even easier, as in the case of Hebrews. Gradually, such local churches must have not only borrowed the precious letters, but also made, painfully slowly, copies for themselves. So, by degrees, their little stock of 'New Testament' books would have grown; for the Old Testament they had already. But, of course, the stock of books would be different in different areas; and what were they to do if some group of false teachers appeared with a forged letter? That such forgeries existed, we can see from Paul's words in 2 Thessalonians 2: 2.

□ A Later Series

Are there any parallels outside the New Testament? Yes, there are, in the early history of the Christian Church. Early in the second century after Christ, a valiant, if somewhat unbalanced, bishop from Antioch was sent to Rome for execution. His name was Ignatius. On his journey to Rome, he wrote a series of letters to the various churches of the area, whose problems he knew so well. His letters do not of course claim to be inspired; and in places their theology is frankly different from that of his greatly-admired Paul. But nevertheless, after his death, these letters were reverently gathered together and preserved, as we may suppose those of Paul to have been, two generations before.

□ Four Portraits of Christ

What of the Gospels? Here the process is less clear: but, by the time that the collection of Paul's letters has begun to appear, so has the collection of the four Gospels. There are numerous ways in which we can prove this, but they are rather technical for a book of this nature; any of the standard introductions to the New Testament will discuss the question. We have already seen something of the probable way in which the four Gospels came into being; and, once there, they seem to have won universal acceptance. They, in later days, fulfilled a function even more necessary than that of the Letters: for only there could men find a reliable account of the Jesus Whom they worshipped. Gone were the first generation of eye-witnesses; but here was their witness, embodied in paper and ink, available for reading in worship each Lord's Day. The early Church gave numerous reasons for there being four, and only four, Gospels. For instance, they said, there are only four winds, only four points of the compass—and so on. But the plain meaning of this is that they were trying to explain the existence of something that was there already, in the shape of the Four Gospels.

□ The Pocket Library Complete

What of the rest of the New Testament? With Paul's Letters and the four Gospels fixed as nucleus, the rest probably grouped itself naturally around them. The Acts was a natural accompaniment; and the Letters by other apostles (in which we may include Revelation, because of its opening section) would be preserved in the areas where these had worked. All is associated with the first generation: indeed, it is probable that no book was included in the New Testament unless it was believed to be by an apostle—or, at least, to rest on the testimony of an apostle.

□ Rejected Numbers

Were there any other books, other than those included in our 'New Testament'? Yes, indeed, there were; and it was precisely because of their appearance that it became necessary for the early Christians to decide what was inside the 'New Testament', and what was outside it. Even before the ending of the age of the Gospels and Letters, we see the rise of heresy within the Church; the Book of Revelation and the Letters of John contain the clearest references to it, though hints appear in various parts of Paul's Letters too. This group was later called

'The Know-Alls', or Gnostics, from the Greek word for 'knowledge'. They despised the 'simple' faith of the ordinary Christian, and usually claimed to have had fresh revelations themselves—and often produced the new books they had written as evidence. When they began attaching the names of well-known apostles and leaders of the primitive Church to these forged books, the simple Christian was confused. But one thing he knew 'in his bones': these were not the same as the other 'holy books' that they treasured.

□ The Reason for Rejection

So it became necessary to list the 'holy Scriptures', in distinction to these. Not every local church, in those far-off days, would have the same lists, but the nucleus they would all share in common. By degrees, the books 'around the edges', as it were, were either included or excluded, according as they were perceived to be inspired or not. That this was not the opinion of a group of theological specialists, but the mind of the whole Church, can be easily and simply proved. It is possible today, in most public libraries, to get a copy of what is often called 'The Apocryphal New Testament', a collection of these excluded books. If you read this, or a part of this, you will see that it is as different from our New Testament as salt water is from fresh. This process of sifting and approving is called 'the formation of the Canon'. ('Canon' here means something like 'an approved list'.) The important thing to realise is that it was not 'the Church giving us the Bible', as is some-sometimes said. It was the Church recognising the Bible as the Word of God; and that is a very different thing.

7 USING THE LIBRARY

□ Thumbing Through the Books

Now that we have considered the various books in this Christian Library, we come to the most vital question of all: how should we best use it? One humorist once said that the greatest barrier to Bible study was the great number of books about the Bible. He did not mean that they were necessarily bad books: far from it—but, the better the book, the greater the danger that we will read it instead of the Bible itself. But, of course, we can never get to know the Bible by reading books about the Bible, helpful though these may be. We shall only get to know the Bible by reading the Bible itself. Now, how shall we do this, especially with reference to the New Testament? We are not speaking now of any of the many excellent systems of reading the Bible devotionally and systematically, day by day. But, if this book has achieved anything of its purpose, you will now want to read something of the New Testament as a whole, in addition.

□ Where should we Start?

What book should we read first? This may not seem a very important question to you as you sit in a comfortable chair at home, but it is a very real one to the missionary, as he ponders over the problem of which book to translate first, which book to teach the convert to read first. On the other hand, if you are an adult convert, coming from a pagan background, you may see the relevance of this at once. Well, naturally we should turn at once to the story of Christ Himself: that was the path by which we entered the Kingdom, just as all our spiritual forefathers did. Usually, people have begun with Mark (as simplest) or Luke (as most full of human interest), and read through it steadily and prayerfully, but not breaking it up into tiny fragments, as the various daily reading systems must do. When you have read a section—in a modern translation, if you find it clearer—then shut your eyes and prayerfully meditate upon what you have read. Try to imagine how it must have been for someone who heard this news for the first time. If you are a Hebrew convert, you will prefer Matthew; philosophers will turn at once to John; but most of us will tackle these books later.

□ Why not with Acts?

But, supposing that you are already fairly familiar with the main events in the life of

Christ, it is a more exciting adventure, as suggested above, to begin with the Acts of the Apostles. After all, that is where all the early Christian Church (except the apostles themselves) started. Begin by analysing those early speeches by Peter; trace your own experience of the gospel in them. Then follow the spiritual life of the Jerusalem church, up to the conversion of Paul; that makes a natural break. See how your own early joys and sorrows, failures and successes, are all mirrored in those pages; everything is still so fresh and new and wonderful in the Christian life. When you have read over and over again, then you may like to turn to the Letter of James to see the moral strength of a church like that: unimaginative, dry, and dour—but sterling Christian character. If you want to see the awful temptations that assailed a church like this, see the Letter to the Hebrews: should they go back to Judaism after all? But how can they go back? If you want to know the sort of gospel that such a church found the very strength of its life, read slowly through the Gospel of Matthew; if you want to see the warnings that Christians received, look at the Letter of Jude.

□ Some Bigoted Christians

This sort of 'consecutive' study will prove very rewarding: James, and the elders of Jerusalem, will be like old friends; you can see their strength and love them. But can you see their weaknesses too, and still love them? You must read on in the Acts of the Apostles for that; for it was not the church of Jerusalem that brought the gospel to the ends of the earth: it was, by the grace of God, Paul, the 'overseas Jew', supported by the rowdy cheerful Gentile church of Antioch. One group in the Jerusalem church (that connected with the Pharisees, Acts 15: 5, and probably also with the priests, Acts 6: 7) actually became Paul's bitterest enemies, and did all in their power to thwart him. The 'Judaisers', as they are called, felt that a man could only become a Christian, if he was prepared to be circumcised, and keep all the ritual law of the Jews (Acts 15: 1). This Paul violently opposed, as a 'false gospel' (Galatians 1: 6). Of course, Acts is clear that James himself did not fall into this error (Acts 15: 24), but it was the great danger of his group, with its narrow horizons.

□ Branch-line Churches

But this Jerusalem church, though interesting and pathetic, is more of a warning to us than an example. In any case, it was not 'main-line,' but a 'siding': after Jerusalem had fallen twice, and when all Jews had finally been expelled from Palestine by the exasperated Romans in the mid-second century, it came to an end. The main line is that pioneered by Paul—the Gentile churches that God used him to found. Most of us will find their outlook, and problems, and difficulties, surprisingly 'contemporary', and close to ours. There were, however, other early streams of Jewish Christianity, besides that of Jerusalem—streams that flowed more readily into the main current. John represents one of these: if we turn to his Gospel and Letters, they will make a fruitful study in themselves. Here we can meditate for long without exhausting the riches. Peter represents another: after we have read either his speeches in Acts, or the Gospel of Mark, or perhaps both, we can study his appearances in the Acts of the Apostles. He is still the same dear, lovable, inconsistent Peter: sometimes he comes very near to being caught up in the Judaising heresy, as in Galatians 2: 11–14. Always, however, there is repentance and renewal for Peter; and we can turn then to his two Letters to see his pastor's heart. If tradition is right, he shared a martyr's death with Paul at Rome: we may like to meditate again on John 20: 18.

□ The Acts of Paul

All of these, even Jerusalem, are 'tributaries' of the main stream: but the main stream is undoubtedly that represented by Paul, and we shall want to spend most of our time studying this. All the second part of the Book of Acts is really the Acts of

Paul—or rather the acts of the Spirit through Paul, and the bulk of the Letters in the New Testament are from his pen. That Paul actually knew Luke's Gospel is unlikely; but, if Acts was written after the Gospel (as seems clear), and if Acts was written in Paul's lifetime (which is likely), then at least he could have known the material in it. It is interesting to speculate whether Luke may not have been gathering the material for his Gospel while in Jerusalem, possibly in Paul's company: for clearly he depends on eye-witnesses from Palestine. In any case, Paul shows knowledge of some of the events of Christ's life; and the form is a typically 'Lukan' one—see 1 Corinthians 11: 23–25. This Gospel of Luke clearly expresses the mind of this section of the Church.

☐ Missionary Letters

From now on, we can have a thrilling spiritual experience. As we read the Acts, and the missionary preaching of Paul in each place, sometimes we can see the nature of his approach. But we can also turn back ourselves to Luke's Gospel, and ask ourselves the question: what are the sort of stories from this 'Gospel for the Gentiles' that would have been appropriate here? For, if Paul did not use them, we can be sure that Luke or other later Gentile preachers did. This is, however, only the beginning: we can, in many cases, turn to the Letters that Paul later sent to these selfsame churches, and see how their spiritual life wavered. We can see all the practical problems that confronted them (many, as we have said, the same as confront us, though in modern dress). We may even like to see the origins of some of these problems in the circumstances of their evangelism, as told in Acts itself. If we really enter into this, we will feel over these first-century converts as Paul did: which of them is weak, and do we not, in sympathetic imagination, share that weakness (2 Corinthians 11: 29)? Like him, we shall feel ourselves 'in labour' over these pathetic little groups, so lovable and yet so weak (Galatians 4: 19). Deepest of all, we shall not only see our local church in them: we shall see, all too clearly, ourselves.

□ An Absorbing Study

By now, Bible study will have become to us not only a deepening spiritual experience, but an absorbing pursuit. We shall feel ourselves almost cheated—as though we had been reading an exciting book, of which the last chapters have been torn out, so that we do not know the end. What happened to these churches afterwards? Did Corinth, for instance, respond to Paul? How did Ephesus fare, where he worked so long? And his old 'home base', Antioch— did it keep its missionary vision bright? To know the answer to some of these, we can turn to the 'Pastoral

93

Epistles', the Letters to Timothy and Titus. Clouds are over the horizon; the veteran warrior sees the persecutions that are to come. More, he sees already the first signs of heresies; and, wise warrior as he is, he takes all the precautions that he can. Even as we notice the deteriorating conditions, within and without, note the different steps that he takes: we may yet need to take them.

□ The Sequel

This is just before the 'grand old man' passes away, after fighting his good fight (2 Timothy 4: 7). But what happened after that? Did, perhaps, his martyrdom change these churches at last? No: we have information in the New Testament of the churches of at least one area, after Paul's death. Revelation 1–3 shows us conditions in the 'Seven Churches' of West Turkey, the very area where Paul had laboured long (Acts 19: 10) and to which he had written many rich letters (Galatians, Ephesians, Colossians, Philemon, and the lost 'Laodiceans'). With a shock, we find that we might be reading a description of church life in our lands today. Here are men who have lost their first love (Revelation 2: 4); here are groups who have the name of being alive, and yet are spiritually dead (3: 1); here are lukewarm churches (3: 16); here are churches that care more about worldly wealth than spiritual riches (3: 17). Persecution, immorality, heresy—all these are vexing the sorely-tried little groups. Yet, in every place, there are also those who are still faithful, still enduring, although they are pitifully weak (3:8); and to these comes God's promise of ultimate triumph. Indeed, it is for such as these that the Book of Revelation is written: for we must not forget that it is directed to the same group of Seven Churches as the letters in the first three chapters; and so, as we read the book, we can think lovingly of them as well as ourselves.

☐ *Act Two*

What if we want to take the study still further? Then Bible study becomes the study of Church history: and, although no Church history is inspired, yet you will find it an inspiring study too. When you feel that you have chewed and digested the Biblical material about these early churches, then see what we know of them in later days—Rome, Corinth, Ephesus, Antioch, Jerusalem, and the others. We can find out something about most of these in the works of the 'Apostolic Fathers', the group of Christian worthies who came immediately after the days of the New Testament. We can find out much more about them in the days of the later Church historians, who began to write a couple of hundred years later. So often, these churches still show the characteristics that marked them in Biblical days—Corinth is still noisy, Rome is still orderly.

☐ The End of the Whole Matter

And so it comes almost as a shock to us to realise that the men in New Testament days whom the Spirit used were ordinary, not supermen. One of the greatest of English scholar-bishops used to continually warn his classes against the danger of unconsciously clothing the early centuries of Christian history with light. If we do that, we shall utterly fail to realise that New Testament Letter and Gospel alike were written to men and churches just as weak and sinful as we are. Yet if we fail to realise that, we shall not dare to apply the promises and encouragements to ourselves, as well as the warnings, and so the Bible will not seem relevant. This is the devil's last and greatest weapon: if he cannot make the Christian doubt the Bible, he will stop the Christian from using the Bible—and this is one of the most subtle ways. But the message of the Bible is plain: 'Elijah was a man of like nature with ourselves, and he prayed fervently that it might not rain, and . . . it did not rain' (James 5: 17, R.S.V.). God's miracles are ever wrought by Him through and for ordinary men and women like ourselves; today, too, with Him, nothing is impossible (Matthew 19: 26). If we read the Bible with these truths in mind, God will do miracles again in our age; and God Himself knows how sorely we need them—but no more sorely, as we have seen, than the Church of the New Testament did.